D1224380

You Know You're Really Pregnant When...

You Know You're Really Pregnant When...

By Lisa Emmett Arnold

PRICE STERN SLOAN
Los Angeles

Copyright © 1987 by Lisa Emmett Arnold
Published by Price Stern Sloan, Inc.
360 North La Cienega Boulevard, Los Angeles, California 90048

Printed in the United States of America. All rights reserved. No part of this
publication may be reproduced, stored in a retrieval system or transmitted,
in any form or by any means, electronic, mechanical, photocopying, recording
or otherwise, without the prior written permission of the publishers.
ISBN: 0-8431-1916-0
10 9 8 7 6 5 4 3 2

for Ron...

You know you're really pregnant when...

you leave the doctor's office and call everyone you know.

You know you're really pregnant when...

*you buy a stretchie
for the first time.*

You know you're really pregnant when...

your extra room suddenly has a crib in it.

You know you're really pregnant when...

you think about using your high heels for planters.

You know you're really pregnant when...

people keep asking you if you've put on weight.

You know you're really pregnant when...

you actually get a seat on the bus.

You know you're really pregnant when...

you begin to refer to yourself as "we."

You know you're really pregnant when...

morning sickness lasts all day and night.

You know you're really pregnant when...

you suddenly can't stand the smell of your favorite perfume.

You know you're really pregnant when...

you only get to watch the top half of your favorite soap.

You know you're really pregnant when...

you need attention ALL of the time.

You know you're really pregnant when...

you cry buckets of tears, and no one tells you to snap out of it.

You know you're really pregnant when...

you know where every bathroom is in the store.

You know you're really pregnant when…

you stop trying to hold your tummy in.

You know you're really pregnant when...

your doctor becomes angel-like in your eyes.

You know you're really pregnant when…

what you wished for in seventh grade actually happens.

You know you're really pregnant when…

salespeople start showing you dresses that have giant bows and ruffles around the collar.

You know you're really
pregnant when...

*your mate doesn't care if
you try to flirt at a party.*

You know you're really pregnant when...

you begin to hate flights of stairs almost as much as you hate string bikinis.

You know you're really pregnant when…

elastic maternity pants no longer make you wince.

You know you're really pregnant when…

people talk to your stomach.

You know you're really pregnant when...

you've already chosen the baby's name, but your relatives still give you "what to name the baby" books.

You know you're really pregnant when...

you tie your bathrobe WAY above your waist.

You know you're really pregnant when...

you go to Lamaze class, and everyone looks just like you!

You know you're really pregnant when…

your biggest "big dress" now fits you like a glove.

You know you're really pregnant when...

you get stuck between tables in chic cafes.

You know you're really pregnant when...

you begin to waddle.

You know you're really pregnant when...

bending over to tie your sneakers becomes impossible.

You know you're really pregnant when...

you finally have a baby!